Where Is Everybody?

Where Is Everybody?

AN ANIMAL ALPHABET BY
Eve Merriam

WITH ILLUSTRATIONS BY
Diane de Groat

SIMON & SCHUSTER BOOKS FOR YOUNG READERS
Published by Simon & Schuster
New York • London • Toronto • Sydney • Tokyo • Singapore

To my two favorite photographers in the world,
Ellen and Pam

—Eve Merriam

For my niece, Julie Soller,
because she knows a vicuna when she sees one

—Diane de Groat

SIMON & SCHUSTER BOOKS FOR YOUNG READERS
Simon & Schuster Building, Rockefeller Center
1230 Avenue of the Americas, New York, New York 10020.

Text copyright © 1989 by Eve Merriam
Illustrations copyright © 1989 by Diane de Groat
All rights reserved including the right of reproduction in whole
or in part in any form.
SIMON & SCHUSTER BOOKS FOR YOUNG READERS
is a trademark of Simon & Schuster.
Designed by Mary Ahern
Manufactured in the United States of America

10 9 8 7 6 5 4 3 2

(pbk) 10 9 8 7 6 5 4 3 2

Library of Congress Cataloging-in-Publication Data
Merriam, Eve.
Where is everybody? : an animal alphabet.
SUMMARY: A humorous alphabet of animals engaged in human
activities, including an alligator in the attic, a unicorn
underwater, and an elephant riding on the escalator.
1. English language—Alphabet—Juvenile literature   2. Animals—
Juvenile literature.   [1. Alphabet.   2. Animals.]   I. De Groat, Diane, ill.
II. Title   PE1155.M48   1989   88-19800
ISBN 0-671-64964-7   ISBN 0-671-77821-8 (pbk)

A lligator is in the attic.

B ear is in the bakery.

C at is at the computer.

Dog is at the daycare center.

E lephant is on the escalator.

Frog is in the factory.

Giraffe is in the garage.

H

ippopotamus is in the hardware store.

I bex is on the ice.

J aguar is on the jungle gym.

Kangaroo is in the kitchen.

L ion is in the laundry room.

M onkey is in the market.

 arwhal is in the noodle house.

O wl is in the opera.

P enguin is in the Post Office.

Quail is on the quarterdeck.

R

abbit is on the roller coaster.

Sheep is in the stroller.

Tiger is in the taxi.

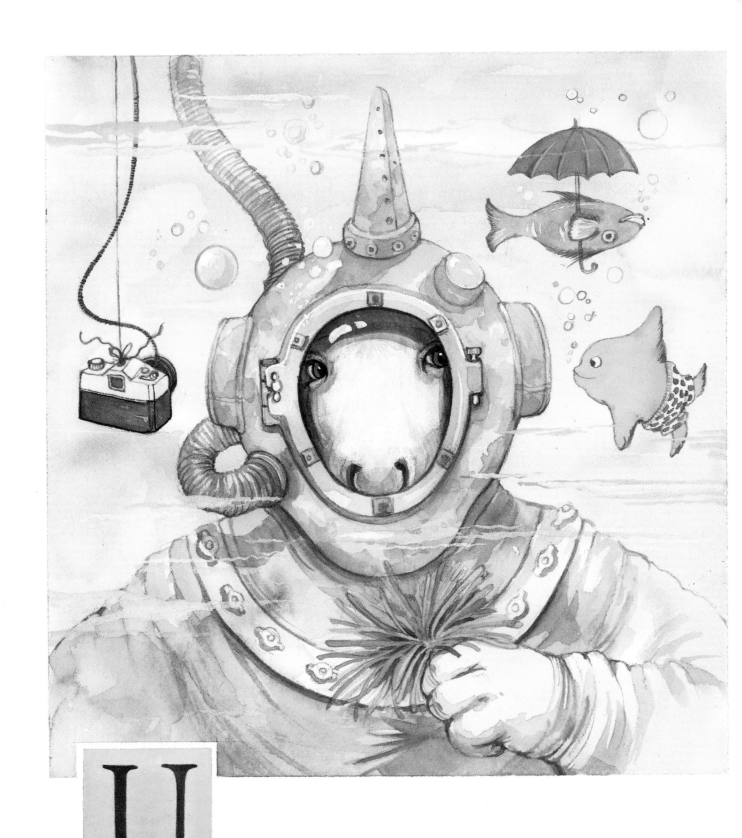

U

nicorn is underwater.

Vicuna is at the video store.

Walrus is at the wheel.

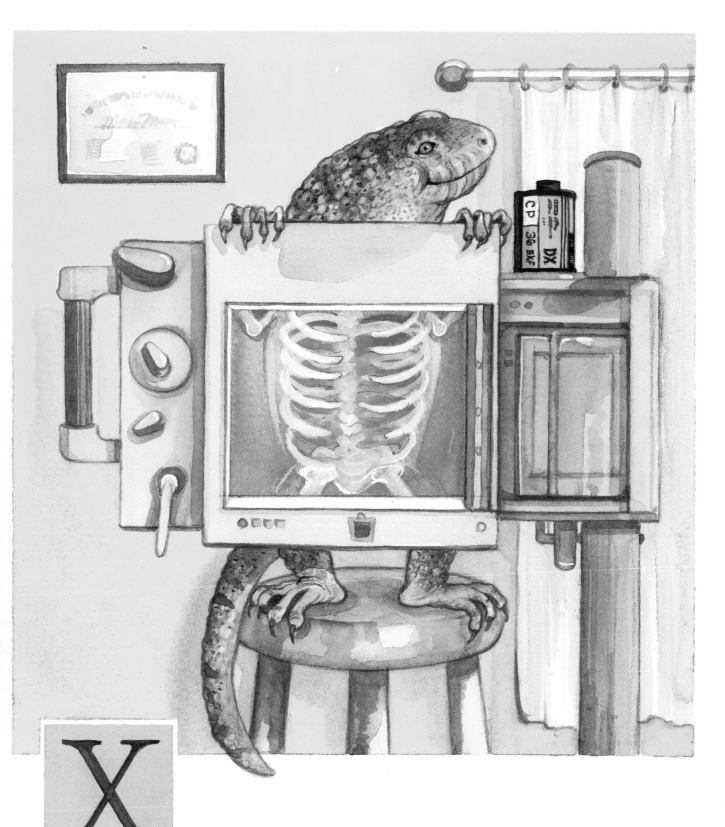

X enosaurid is at the X-ray machine.

Yak is in the yard.

Zebra is at the zoo.

DATE DUE

JAN. 0 2 1996		
MAR. 1 2 1995		
MAY 2 2 1995		
AUG 2 8 '96		
OCT 0 2 '96		
SEP 2 8 '97		
OCT 1 9 '97		
OCT 0 1 '99		
OCT 0 5		
MAR 2 2 2001		
OCT 1 4 2001		
MAR 2 4 2002		
MAR 3 0 2002		
JAN 0 2 2003		
OCT 2 7 2003		PRINTED IN U.S.

GAYLORD